Joseph Sinasac

NOVALIS

John Paull

Santo Subito!

During Pope John Paul II's
funeral on April 8, 2005, the
emotional crowd cried out,
"Santo subito!" — "Make him a
saint, now!" Only six years later
— lightning speed for Rome —
he has been beatified, becoming
Blessed John Paul II on May 1,
2011, a major milestone on the
road to canonization.

His life was touched by many of the great movements and tragedies of the 20th century. During his more than eight decades on earth, he was personally marked by the rise of Nazism, the Second World War, and Soviet-style Communism, which held his beloved Poland in thrall for almost half a century. He was a bishop at the Second Vatican Council and helped bring its spirit alive in his own archdiocese of Krakow.

Saint Mary's church in Krakow, Poland.
Built in the 16th century, its asymmetrical
facade dominates the Old Town Square.
For many centuries it has been regarded
as the most important church in the city.
The lower tower houses five bells,
while the higher tower has served as a
watchtower since the Middle Ages.
A trumpeter plays the Hejnal
every hour on the hour.

The early years

John Paul II's early life was
rooted in the provincial Polish
town of Wadowice, a busy
community of about 10,000 with
a vibrant cultural life. Karol
Wojtyla was born May 18, 1920,
to Karol Sr., a non-commissioned
army officer, and his wife,
Emilia. Karol Jr. was the second
son and third child, though his
older sister had died shortly
after her birth. His older
brother, Edmund, was almost
14 years his senior and would
become a doctor by the time
young Karol was 10.

Karol's father retired from the army in 1927. The family was far from rich, living a frugal middle-class existence on the military pension supplemented by income from his mother's sewing and embroidery. Tragedy struck early in Karol's life when his sickly mother died in 1929; Karol was only in third grade.

From then until he entered university, Karol depended heavily on his father, imbibing from him a deep piety. Prayer, the rosary and Scripture reading were standard practices in the Wojtyla household.

In his late teens and early 20s, Karol was absorbed by the stage and appeared to be headed for a career as an actor. He and his father moved to Krakow in 1938 so Karol Jr. could study at Jagiellonian University, a centre of ancient learning, where Copernicus had studied. In addition to his studies in languages and literature, Karol indulged his love for the stage, taking part in campus productions.

War changes everything

September 1, 1939, was the day
Adolf Hitler's blitzkrieg first
demonstrated its brutal
effectiveness — the day
Germany invaded Poland and
began the Second World War.

For young Karol, life as he knew it came to an abrupt end. On that morning, Karol, now a second-year university student, was serving Mass at Wawel Cathedral in Krakow. The gathered congregation could hear the warning sirens, followed by exploding bombs and anti-aircraft guns. As soon as Mass was over, Karol hastened home to his father.

For the next five-and-a-half years, until the war's end, Poland would suffer as no other country would from the ravages of the Third Reich, which terrorized two-thirds of the country, leaving the other third to Stalin's Red Army. Poland's population was decimated. It was also the site of some of the worst horrors of the Jewish Holocaust.

Within a year, Karol found himself working as forced labour in a quarry, though he continued his studies with the help of former professors who had started underground classes.

During these years, Karol was introduced to contemplative prayer and some of the Church's great mystics, especially St. John of the Cross, whose writings were to have a lasting influence on his life. Another book, *True Devotion to the Blessed Virgin Mary*, by St. Louis de Montfort, would later provide the new Pope with his motto, *Totus Tuus* (I am all yours).

Alas, Karol's father died on February 18, 1941, leaving a gaping hole in the life of his 20-year-old son. His father's death became a turning point in Karol's life. "A light was beginning to shine ever more brightly in the back of my mind: the Lord wants me to become a priest," the eventual Pope wrote in *Gift and Mystery* in 1996.

Until that moment, acting still seemed the most likely career choice for Karol. Now he was torn between acting and the priesthood. In the fall of 1942, Karol made up his mind.

He was accepted as a seminarian by a pleased Adam Stefan Sapieha, archbishop of Krakow. As the Nazis cracked down on the Church, Karol and the other seminarians were forced to move into the archbishop's residence, which became a secret seminary. But he almost didn't make it. On one Gestapo sweep of Krakow, Karol was forced to hide behind a basement door in a friend's apartment, narrowly escaping the Germans, who searched the other two floors of the building.

With the help of a friend, he hastened to the archbishop's palace, where he remained for the rest of his seminary studies as one of Sapieha's "secretaries."

Karol's seminary studies were finished a year after the war ended. He was ordained to the priesthood for the archdiocese of Krakow on November 1, 1946.

The young priest

Archbishop Sapieha's first
assignment for Fr. Wojtyla
was more studies, this time
in Rome. After studying at
the Angelicum (the Pontifical
University of St. Thomas
Aquinas), he returned to Poland,
to the theology faculty at the
Jagiellonian, where he received
his doctorate in theology in 1948.

As a young priest, Fr. Wojtyla, though he had plenty of friends and social activity, led a life of personal ascetism. He had next to no money, had no bank account and gave away most of his possessions. He wore second-hand cassocks and old shoes. He also maintained a heavy regimen of disciplined prayer.

After obtaining his second
doctorate in 1954 from the
Jagiellonian faculty of theology,
Fr. Wojtyla joined the Catholic
University of Lublin as a
member of the faculty of
philosophy. He was a popular
professor, always approachable
outside of class, and could
often be found in prayer
in the chapel.

Krakow, a beautiful Polish
city that was once the capital.
This view is of the main market square.

Life as a bishop

Perhaps it was inevitable that
on September 28, 1958, at
age 38, he became the youngest
bishop in Poland as auxiliary
for Krakow.

In 1958, Fr. Wojtyla had been
out on a kayaking expedition
with friends when he got a call
to return to the city. He hurried
back, changed into clerical
garb and presented himself
to Cardinal Stefan Wyszynski,
the primate of Poland. Cardinal
Wyszynski told him he was to be
made a bishop. After accepting
the appointment, he spent the
better part of a day in prayer
before returning to his friends,
who were camping along a
riverbank.

Early in his new career,
Bishop Wojtyla participated
in a historical event in the
life of the Catholic Church.
On January 25, 1959, Pope
John XXIII announced plans
for the Second Vatican Council,
which would bring together
the world's bishops to "open
the windows" of the Church
to the modern world.

During the four Council sessions (1962–65), Bishop Wojtyla became spokesman for the Polish bishops and was placed on a commission studying population, family and birth issues. He also became a member of the committee that drafted *Gaudium et Spes* (Pastoral Constitution on the Church in the Modern World), one of the most important documents of the 16 the Council produced.

To the end of his life, Pope John Paul II used the teachings of Vatican II as the starting point for his own writing, peppering his paragraphs with quotes from the Council documents and framing his own thoughts in what he believed was the true spirit of the Second Vatican Council.

Bishop Wojtyla also became
one of the first bishops to bring
the spirit of Vatican II home.
By the end of the Council,
he was archbishop of Krakow,
having been elevated to the
see on December 30, 1963.

Pope Paul VI made Archbishop Wojtyla a cardinal on October 14, 1967. By this time, he was immersed in renewing spiritual life in Krakow and beginning to see other parts of the world. A cardinal, particularly one as eloquent and insightful as he, was in great demand to speak throughout the world.

Papabili

To understand the election of
Pope John Paul II, we first
need to consider the conclave
of August 25-26, 1978, where
his predecessor, John Paul I,
was elected.

Pope Paul VI had died on the evening of Sunday, August 6. In remarkably short order, the gathered cardinals elected Cardinal Albino Luciani, patriarch of Venice. At age 65, Cardinal Luciani had gained a sizable following for his simple holiness, warmth and superior communication skills.

John Paul I quickly won the hearts of Italians and Catholics around the world with his humility and compassion.

But, unknown to those who elected him, his health was not up to the task. Thirty-four days after his election, he was dead of natural causes.

Cardinal Wojtyla had been present at the August conclave and was in attendance when the cardinals gathered once again to choose a pope on October 14. This time there was a belief that the next pope should be someone fresh and healthy, certainly from outside the curia and perhaps even from outside Italy. Cardinal Wojtyla, an athletic 58, had already impressed many of his colleagues with his obvious communication skills, his pastoral success in Krakow and his intellectual prowess.

In the end, the cardinal from Poland was elected Pope. Though he had toyed momentarily with choosing the name Stanislaus, he opted for the name John Paul II.

A new papacy; a new Church

The words now have become a common refrain. But on October 22, 1978, they rang in the Italian air with vibrant freshness, delivered confidently by the spiritual leader of the world's Catholics, in the prime of his life: "Be not afraid. Open wide the doors for Christ." These two sentences, spoken during the homily of his inauguration Mass in St. Peter's Square before 300,000 people, became seminal themes of the pontificate of Pope John Paul II.

These words ushered in a new era for the Church. It wasn't long before the Pope began to display the energy, charisma, creativity and zeal that would become his trademarks.

On January 25, 1979, he embarked on the first of many international trips, taking in Mexico, the Dominican Republic, and the Bahamas.

There would be four such trips that year, including historic visits to his native Poland, where he challenged the Communist regime with his unapologetic demand that the officially atheistic regime make room for religious faith.

"It is not possible to understand the history of the Polish nation without Christ," he insisted during a homily at Victory Square in Warsaw. The visit was a shot across the bow to the Communist Eastern Bloc, a warning that this Pope may not have tanks at his command, but he held something far more powerful. The Pope became a key figure in the background as Poland began the movement that would throw off the shackles of Soviet domination.

Less than six weeks after his visit, the Gdansk shipyard strike gave birth to the Solidarity trade union. He would be seen as a key figure in the fall of the Berlin Wall in 1989.

An appeal to Our Lady

May 13, 1981, almost brought all
the promise of this new energetic
Pope to an end. At 5:19 p.m.,
Turkish terrorist Mehmet Ali
Agca, 23, was waiting behind a
pillar in St. Peter's Square.
When the Pope came by in his
Popemobile, Agca jumped out
and fired twice from his
Browning 9-mm semi-automatic
pistol. The bullet ripped through
the Pope's abdomen, causing
extensive damage and massive
bleeding.

After six hours of surgery, he emerged alive and on the road to recovery. But it was an incredibly close call. Pope John Paul credited Our Lady of Fatima with saving his life that day. And he forgave his would-be assassin: "I pray for that brother of ours who shot me, and whom I have sincerely pardoned."

View of St. Peter's Square in Rome, as seen from the top of the Vatican.

Taking care of business

In his early years, Pope John Paul aggressively attacked what he saw as problems within Church institutions. In one of his most far-reaching decisions, he appointed Cardinal Joseph Ratzinger, a German theologian, as prefect of the Congregation for the Doctrine of the Faith on November 25, 1981, setting one of the Church's leading lights on his own path to the papacy.

Interior of St. Peter's Basilica in Rome.

O Canada

Considering the vast travels of the Pope, it was inevitable that he would eventually end up in Canada. But his 12-day visit in September 1984 was no ordinary occasion for this country's Catholics. First of all, it was the first visit to Canada by any pope. In cities across Canada, he delivered speeches that dealt with issues such as living in a technological age, secularism and — repeatedly — the need to address the long-standing grievances of Canada's Aboriginal peoples.

In his discussions with Native peoples, the Pope's comments were a precursor of his later apologies on behalf of the Church for its failings throughout history. He admitted that the Church had committed "blunders" in the way it had evangelized indigenous peoples and had failed to respect their cultures.

He insisted that First Nations were "full-fledged members of the Church, although not of society."

Youth of the World

One of the most popular
initiatives of Pope John Paul
was his embrace of the youth
of the world. In 1985, the Pope
issued his own apostolic letter,
To the Youth of the World.
In the letter, he addressed
youth directly and sought to
understand their problems,
all the while inviting them
to be full players in the People
of God.

The Pope also urged youth not
to give away the sexual aspect
of their personality cheaply.
"Do not be afraid of the love
that places clear demands
on people. These demands...
are precisely capable of making
your love a true love."

This was also the year of the first official World Youth Day, held in Rome on Palm Sunday. About 250,000 youth met for that first event and have been celebrating it in countries around the world every few years since then.

From Rome, World Youth Day has travelled to Argentina, Spain, Poland, the United States, the Philippines, France, Canada (in 2002), Germany, Australia, and back to Spain (2011). Millions of young Catholics have gathered at these events to worship God and come to know their faith in companionship with the Pope.

Reaching out

Youth were not the only identifiable group with which the Pope sought to build bridges. Other Christian denominations and even non-Christian faiths were approached. Once again, the Pope underlined the special place he held for the Jewish faith when, on April 13, 1986, he made an unprecedented visit to Rome's main synagogue.

And on October 27 of that year, he took part in the first World Day of Prayer for Peace, which he convened at Assisi. It was attended by representatives of 60 Christian and non-Christian religions.

A teaching Pope

Besides his travels, John Paul
was also the most prolific pope
in history. He regularly
published encyclicals, letters,
exhortations and messages that
fleshed out his view of the
meaning of salvation and the
role of the Christian in history.

His sixth encyclical, *Mother of the Redeemer*, for instance, explored the Pope's lifelong devotion to Mary, whose life he described as an image of obedience and a model of "femininity with dignity."

On the centennial of the great social encyclical of Pope Leo XIII, *Rerum Novarum,* promulgated in 1891, the Pope issued *Centesimus Annus,* which expanded the Church's understanding of the dignity of the human being and the need for social structures to serve humanity, not the other way around. The 1991 encyclical was equally critical of both Communist and capitalist ideologies.

But one of the Pope's most significant enterprises on clarifying Church teaching was the publication of the *Catechism of the Catholic Church* in 1992. This summary of doctrine and practice — translated into all the world's major languages — quickly became a best-seller and was widely accepted as a dependable reference book.

In 1994 he published *Crossing the Threshold of Hope,* a book of questions and answers on faith posed to the Pope by an Italian journalist. It, too, became a global best-seller, being translated into 21 languages and published in 35 countries.

A signal document in the Pope's teaching was published in March 1995. *Evangelium Vitae* (The Gospel of Life) describes a world in which a "culture of death" marked by relativism, materialism and a lack of moral virtue battled with a "culture of life" as expressed by the Gospels and the Church.

These two phrases found their way into common parlance; even U.S. President George W. Bush used the "culture of life" in his State of the Union address in 2005.

The Great Jubilee

As the dawn of the third
millennium approached, Pope
John Paul began to lay out
the steps that were to mark one
of the most remarkable years
in the history of Christendom.
The year 2000 was designed to
kickstart what the Pope liked
to call the "new evangelization."

Though he called it "new," he acknowledged that in many countries with Christian histories, it was an attempt to re-evangelize Christians who had fallen away from the practice of their faith. The Pope often lamented that many lived "lives of practical atheism," or acted as if God did not exist, though they may be nominal Christians.

The year 2000 was full of special occasions. About once a month there were special Masses for different groups within the Church; the first was a Mass for Children in St. Peter's Square on January 2, where the Pope was joined by 150,000 young people. There was also a series of official apologies for those who, acting on behalf of the Church, committed sins during its 2,000-year history.

These apologies began with a special Day of Pardon on the First Sunday of Lent, in which the Church expressed contrition for numerous scandals, including the Inquisition, the treatment of other religions and the Jews.

A year later, the Pope returned to Toronto during World Youth Day 2002 for a week-long extravaganza of faith in one of the world's most secular cities. Some 300,000 gathered at Exhibition Stadium in downtown Toronto to greet the Pope. A few days later, 800,000 gathered at Downsview Park for the final papal Mass.

His work comes to an end

Throughout these final years, the Pope became visibly older and more frail. The Parkinson's disease and arthritis that had long afflicted him began to take their toll. In February 2005, a bout of the flu put the Pope back in the hospital, alarming the world that his death was nigh. But it was apparent to all that this Pope wanted to die in office. As he often said, he would have all eternity to rest.

He saw his own frailty and suffering as a gift from God, one that taught him to understand how the world's people suffered, and to empathize with them. He became a heroic model of self-sacrifice for people around the world.

The final day came on
April 2, 2005.

Through his never-tiring efforts,
the Pope had changed the world
and had challenged us all to be
better than we were, creating
a vision of meaning whose
foundation is in Jesus Christ.
It was a countercultural
example for modern society,
revealing the superficiality and
meaninglessness that filled
our days.

He never stopped praying, never stopped working, never stopped exhorting us to turn to God and be free. Most important of all, he never stopped telling us, "Be not afraid."

Do not be afraid!

Open wide the doors for Christ!

*To his saving power open
the boundaries of states,
economic and political systems,
the vast domains of culture,
civilization and development.*

Do not be afraid!

—Pope John Paul II